FOR A
Smashing
SISTER

summersdale

Summersdale Publishers Ltd
46 West Street
Chichester
West Sussex
PO19 1RP
UK

www.summersdale.com

Printed and bound in China

ISBN: 978-1-84953-340-9

Substantial discounts on bulk quantities of Summersdale books are available to corporations, professional associations and other organisations. For details telephone Nicky Douglas on (+44-1243-756902), fax (+44-1243-786300) or email (nicky@summersdale.com).

To Joanne

From Martha
xxx.

You can kid the world, but not your sister.

CHARLOTTE GRAY

*More than Santa Claus,
your sister knows when
you've been bad and
good.*

LINDA SUNSHINE

Also remember, sisters make the best friends in the world.

MARILYN MONROE

The Wright brothers' sister, Katherine, was responsible for teaching her siblings the mathematics of flight, which was crucial in the invention of the world's first successful aeroplane.

*What's the good of news
if you haven't a sister to
share it?*

JENNY DEVRIES

You're smashing because...

... you've seen me at my best, worst and silliest and don't judge me for it.

The best thing about having a sister was that I always had a friend.

CALI RAE TURNER

To the outside world we all grow old. But not to brothers and sisters.

CLARA ORTEGA

You deserve
an award for:

Never Telling
My Secrets.

Families are the compass that guides us... and our comfort when we occasionally falter.

BRAD HENRY

Having a sister is like having a best friend you can't get rid of.

AMY LI

A study shows those with sisters turn out to be kinder, more giving people. They say one factor for this is that the presence of sisters in a family encourages everybody to be open and talk about their feelings.

Sisters function as safety nets in a chaotic world simply by being there for each other.

CAROL SALINE

You're smashing because...

... you share all the
gossip with me.

*How do people make it
through life without a
sister?*

SARA CORPENING WHITEFORD

Brothers and sisters are as close as hands and feet.

VIETNAMESE PROVERB

You don't choose your family. They are God's gift to you, as you are to them.

DESMOND TUTU

You deserve
an award for:

Being Brutally Honest
when I most need it.

A sister is a gift to the heart, a friend to the spirit, a golden thread to the meaning of life.

ISADORA JAMES

The family is one of nature's masterpieces.

GEORGE SANTAYANA

A sister is a little bit of childhood that can never be lost.

MARION C. GARRETTY

Siblings are the people... who teach us about fairness and cooperation and kindness and caring — quite often the hard way.

PAMELA DUGDALE

*Sisters never quite forgive
each other for what
happened when they
were five.*

PAM BROWN

You're smashing
because...

.... you're always organised
— you know what I'm doing
even when I don't!

In thee my soul shall own combined the sister and the friend.

CATHERINE KILLIGREW

A family in harmony will prosper in everything.

CHINESE PROVERB

You deserve an award for:

Supporting Me when
I'm in trouble.

A ministering angel shall my sister be.

WILLIAM SHAKESPEARE, HAMLET

The family is the country of the heart.

GIUSEPPE MAZZINI

By the age of 11, studies have shown that a child has spent around one-third of their free time with their sibling.

Your siblings are the only people... who know what it's like to have been brought up the way you were.

BETSY COHEN

You're smashing because...

... you're always keen to go shopping with me.

'Help one another' is
part of the religion of
sisterhood.

LOUISA MAY ALCOTT

Sisters are different flowers from the same garden.

ANONYMOUS

Other things may change us, but we start and end with family.

ANTHONY BRANDT

You deserve an award for:

Being a Best Friend,
no matter what.

*A perfect sister I am not,
but thankful for the one
I've got.*

ANONYMOUS

Better to have one woman on your side than ten men.

ROBERT JORDAN

I, who have no sisters or brothers, look with some degree of innocent envy on those who may be said to be born to friends.

JAMES BOSWELL

Never underestimate
the power of sisters.
Among the most famous
suffragettes, who fought
for women's right to vote,
were the Pankhurst sisters:
Christabel, Sylvia and Adela.

Family is the most important thing in the world.

DIANA, PRINCESS OF WALES

You're smashing because...

... you're always happy
to share your things.

A sister can be seen as someone who is both ourselves and very much not. . . a special kind of double.

TONI MORRISON

Women are like teabags.
We don't know our true
strength until we are in
hot water.

ELEANOR ROOSEVELT

*You deserve
an award for:*

Making All of my
Birthdays Extra Special.

Sweet is the voice of a sister in the season of sorrow, and wise is the counsel of those who love us.

BENJAMIN DISRAELI

A true sister is a friend
who listens with her heart.

ANONYMOUS

Famous literary sisters Charlotte, Emily and Anne Brontë — now regarded as writers of great worth and talent — were first published under pseudonyms. At the time, the idea of a female author was frowned upon — hence Anne was published as 'Acton Bell', Charlotte as 'Currer Bell' and Emily as 'Ellis Bell'.

Tears shed for self are tears of weakness, but tears shed for others are a sign of strength.

BILLY GRAHAM

You're smashing because...

... you make sure I'm OK no
matter how far away I am.

I have always drawn strength from being close to home.

ARTHUR ASHE

Our brothers and sisters are there with us from the dawn of our personal stories to the inevitable dusk.

SUSAN SCARF MERRELL

In family life, love is the oil that eases friction, the cement that binds closer together...

EVA BURROWS

You deserve
an award for:

Always Making
Time for Me.

The mildest, drowsiest sister has been known to turn tiger if her sibling is in trouble.

CLARA ORTEGA

Sibling relationships. . .
outlast marriages, survive
the death of parents,
resurface after quarrels
that would sink any
friendship.

ERICA E. GOODE

It was nice growing up with someone like you — someone to lean on, someone to count on... someone to tell on!

ANONYMOUS

Research has shown that having a sister promotes happiness and optimism. This is because sisters are shown to communicate more than brothers, which has a way of comforting the sibling.

We will always be sisters. Our differences may never go away, but neither, for me, will our song.

ELIZABETH FISHEL

You're smashing because...

... you're ready with junk food and an ear to listen when I need it.

*We cannot destroy
kindred: our chains stretch
a little sometimes, but
they never break.*

MARQUISE DE SÉVIGNÉ

An older sister is a friend
and defender — a listener,
conspirator, a counsellor
and a sharer of delights.
And sorrows...

PAM BROWN

You deserve
an award for:

Helping Me Realise
who I am.

Is solace anywhere more comforting than in the arms of sisters?

ALICE WALKER

A sister smiles when one tells one's stories — for she knows where the decoration has been added.

CHRIS MONTAIGNE

Nowadays when you don't get on with your sister you might go a few days without talking, but in Tudor times, when Queen Mary fell out with her sister Princess Elizabeth, she had her locked in the Tower of London.

There is no better friend than a sister. And there is no better sister than you.

ANONYMOUS

You're smashing because...

... you support my passions and dreams, no matter how big or small.

A happy family is but an earlier heaven.

GEORGE BERNARD SHAW

There can be no situation in life in which the conversation of my dear sister will not administer some comfort to me.

MARY WORTLEY MONTAGU

The strength of a family,
like the strength of an
army, is in its loyalty to
each other.

MARIO PUZO

*You deserve
an award for:*

Always Trying to make me feel included with your friends.

A sister shares childhood memories and grown up dreams.

ANONYMOUS

For there is no friend like a sister
In calm or stormy weather;
To cheer one on the tedious way,
To fetch one if one goes astray.

CHRISTINA ROSSETTI, 'GOBLIN MARKET'

How a person's social skills develop depends heavily on how they interact with their brothers and sisters — it is through them that they learn how to regulate their emotions in a socially acceptable way and manage disagreements.

A loyal sister is worth a thousand friends.

MARIAN EIGERMAN

I sustain myself with the love of family.

MAYA ANGELOU

You're smashing because...

... you're the person I can
have the most fun with.

We acquire friends and we make enemies, but our sisters come with the territory.

EVELYN LOEB

A sibling may be the keeper of one's identity, the only person with the keys to one's unfettered, more fundamental self.

MARIAN SANDMAIER

You deserve
an award for:

Being The Person who can make me laugh in any situation — even when I shouldn't!

To have a loving relationship with a sister... is to have a soulmate for life.

VICTORIA SECUNDA

You're smashing because...

... my best memories
are with you.

If you're interested in finding out more about our gift
books, follow us on Twitter: **@Summersdale**

www.summersdale.com